New City College
Learning Resources Centre

||||||||||||||||||||||||||||||

149401

This book is to be returned on or before the last date stamped below or you will be charged a fine

New City College – Tower Hamlets
Learning Resource Centre
Poplar High Street
London E14 0AF
http://library.tower.ac.uk
Poplar: 020 7510 7⎯⎯⎯

GREENWICH EXCHANGE
LONDON

Greenwich Exchange, London

Focus on
Jean Rhys, *Wide Sargasso Sea*
©Anthony Fowles 2008

First published in Great Britain in 2009
All rights reserved

This book is sold subject to the conditions that it shall not,
by way of trade or otherwise, be lent, resold, hired out or
otherwise circulated without the publisher's prior consent
in any form of binding or cover other than that in which it is
published and without a similar condition including this
condition being imposed on the subsequent purchaser.

Printed and bound by imprintdigital.net
Typesetting and layout by Jude Keen, London
Tel: 020 8355 4541
Cover design by December Publications, Belfast
Tel: 028 90286559

Greenwich Exchange Website: www.greenex.co.uk

Cataloguing in Publication Data is available from the
British Library

ISBN: 978-1-906075-34-7

Contents

To Jonathan

1

Our Miss Gwen

It is a truth requiring universal acknowledgement, I believe, that one of the gravest impediments to the delivery of a seamlessly satisfying novel is the ladling in to its creative mix of too crude a dollop of unassimilated autobiography: that the author best serves the fiction by a totally inconspicuous absenting of self from its page-by-page progression.

Such artistic reticence can be surprisingly difficult to discover.

It will take no particularly uncommon reader to compile a list of highly thought of authors, writers of manifest culture and ability, who have succumbed to this sin of self-regard in their own work. Evelyn Waugh, C.P. Snow, A.S. Byatt, Alan Bennett, for example, all strike me as writers who, on occasion, because excited by the level of personal experience in their narratives – "This is what happened to me!" – have allowed themselves to fall victim to a lax species of narcissism. They have failed properly to translate the personal resonance of that experience into a shared, universal significance: "This is how it happens."

Perhaps I may tilt at still loftier windmills. It seems to me that at the very outset of conception both Marcel Proust and Anthony Powell introduced into the monumental chronicles of their respective times an element which precluded either the *Recherche* or *A Dance to the Music of Time* ever enjoying the possibility of equalling *Our Mutual Friend*, say, or *The Possessed* in scale of achievement. The self – Nicholas Jenkins' reticence can be ear-splitting – is always there. This self – the author – comes to patronise the reader. Too often Proust tells the reader what Marcel is thinking at the given time; tells the reader in later revisionist retrospect what he should understand now. The reader is not asked to work hard enough in arriving at his own conclusions so that, served up on a plate, the information arrives pre-digested. In Proust's case, in particular, this results in sustained *longueurs*. The narrowness of the self-cosseting vision induces an inevitable need to recycle prose rhythms as Marcel yet again is driven to, yes, remember past times.

We may emerge from the *Recherche* or *A Dance to the Music of Time* diverted, entertained and instructed. I do not believe we come away enlightened or enhanced. Proust and Powell alike failed to register that while Dickens wrote *David Copperfield* he did not write *The Unfortunate Adventures of the Boy in the Blacking Factory*.

This is not to say, of course, that admirable fiction spun out of personal experience and contemporary observation is an impossibility. On the contrary just such a genesis probably accounts for the majority of novels that endure. A handful of examples that would stand token for the almost endless list we could compile might be: *Pride and Prejudice*; Gore Vidal's *Washington D.C./The Golden Age*; Dawn Powell's Ohio and New York novels; Patrick White's *Riders in the Chariot*; Joyce's *Ulysses*. These, no doubt, will appear of varying overall achievement. But they are adult in the expunging of all traces of the author from the foreground of the narrative and so from our immediate vision. The signposting is not insulting. The reader is set to work.

A popular way of recommending a book (as I remember from times past) used to be: "It will take you out of yourself." It is an attitude not entirely to be derided. Alas, however, there are too many novels that fail to take us out of ourselves because the author has neglected to remove him- or herself from the text at the outset.

Thus it is obliquely – and just possibly contentiously – I come finally to address the subject of this brief study. And on a note of immediate paradox. It is impossible, I would argue, to cite a serious and enduring novelist more devoid of inventive imagination than Jean Rhys. Whether through nature or nurture she would clearly always have been incapable of writing, say, a novel about an upper-middle-class English spinster finding middle-aged solace of a kind in tending the creature comforts of an unsatisfactorily married Gloucestershire curate. She could never have written a grey comedy of outwardly self-possessed and intellectually assured academics leading a chaotically dysfunctional cat's cradle of emotionally entangled private lives. She could not have even written an account of an orphaned girl, rejected by rich relations, acquiring enough intelligence and grit in an early Victorian institution to become not only a competent governess but capable of saving the soul and winning the heart of her romantically disaffected employer.

Such a deduction is implicit, I believe, in any reasonably attentive reading of Jean Rhys' fiction. The work, we can only come to infer, is a form of hindsight to the author's life. Its matter and settings and themes are extremely intense examples of past personal experience revisited. The matter and settings are repetitive and narrow – we read Jean Rhys not for her breadth of vision but for her intensity – and in a kind of reverse of the author's creative process we start to make largely educated guesses as to the life which provided the novels' recurrent subject matter. And yet, first and last, this is a quite irrelevant activity. Jean Rhys' fiction deserves our ongoing attention not as an oblique diary, not as superior gossip, but on account of its artistically created capture upon the page of insights into the universal human condition.

If, then, to accelerate our purpose we briefly set out the main events and watershed moments in Jean Rhys' life, this is not so as to embark upon that crudest approach to literary appreciation ("Widmerpool, you know, is Sir Reginald Manningham-Buller ..." Well, no, he's not, actually. He is a character in a novel). To outline Jean Rhys' life is a prelude to demonstrating how, as an artist, she came to transcend the banalities of personal experience.

Ella Gwendoline Rees Williams ('Jean Rhys' was a *nom de plume* devised by Ford Madox Ford) was born in 1890 in Dominica in the West Indies. Her father had arrived on the island nine years earlier to take up the post of medical officer to one of the island's administrative districts. Like many newly arrived Europeans he was immediately stricken by fever and, not entirely surprisingly, his restoration to health saw him marrying one of his nurses, a Minna Lockhart who came of stock, partly Scottish and almost certainly slightly Creole, that had long been established in Dominica. The current generation of the family were not local aristocrats of the grandee plantation-owning type but neither were they impoverished. Jean was educated not entirely incompetently at a convent school until at the age of sixteen she was sent to the Perse School for Girls in Cambridge. The object of the exercise was to transform her into a fine, upstanding, Edwardian 'gel'.

The intention foundered. Success in a school play left Jean stage-struck. Of her own initiative she contrived to audition for what was soon to become RADA and, incredibly, was awarded a place. It was a short-lived triumph. Two terms into her attendance it seemed evident to her instructors that she would never expunge her West Indian speech rhythms to make room for the cut-glass cadences the 1908 stage considered the *sine qua non* of any fledgeling Ellen Terry. Distraught (in later years she totally deleted this setback from accounts of her life), Jean Rhys retired to lick her wounded *amour propre* in the St Asaph house of the aunt charged with supervising the eighteen-year-old's well-being. There was no question now, of course, but that she would have to return to her Caribbean home. Her mother was insisting upon it. There was absolutely no alternative.

The eighteen-year-old decided there was. Returning to London she blagged herself – there is no other word – a job in the chorus of a touring company version of the current West End hit, *Our Miss Gibbs*. For some eighteen months, the baby in a line of seasoned, cynical chorus girls, she lived that 'change at Crewe' existence endured by any member of such a third-eleven outfit. With throw-away verve she conjures it up with passing vividness in her first full novel:

An odd life. Morose landladies, boiled onion suppers. Bottles of gin in the dressing room. Perpetual manicuring of one's nails in the Sunday train. Perpetual discussions about men. ('Swine, deary, swine.')

When the tour eventually ended she did not go on to similar or better things. She was not 'discovered' – other, that is, than by a man. Before she was twenty years old Jean Rhys, failing to turn into a fine 'gel', had become no better than she should be, the mistress of a fairly typical (but distinctly wealthy) Edwardian 'gentleman'.

For a year or two the man treated her gently and well, keeping her in a manner she would never again be accustomed to. But, inevitably, he threw her over and after the initial shock, one man led to another.

In 1917 the man was Jean Lenglet, French-Dutch, but, perhaps significantly, in London and not engaged in the Great War. Instead he described himself as a *chansonnier* and journalist – which is half-way to saying a charming chancer. The attraction was mutual, and in 1919, perhaps realising that, as she found herself rising thirty, the high summer of her own ability to charm was on the turn, Jean Rhys settled for the stability of marriage and the uncertainty of moving to Paris. For a while, living on their wits, the couple seem to have been happy and supportive of one another. Not even the relatively commonplace tragedy of losing their first-born, a boy, after only three weeks of inadequate post-natal care split the marriage apart. They moved on to Vienna. Lenglet had blagged – yes, it is the only word; it was what they were still young and confidently *louche* enough to do – the position of secretary to a Japanese officer at the Inter-Allied Disarmament Conference in Vienna. This was a Congress which did not so much dance as fiddle. Post-Great War Europe represented a banquet for black-marketeers. The preferred medium was illegal currency transactions. It was Lenglet's preference anyhow. But within two years his rogue-trader chickens were coming home to roost. The Lenglets skipped Vienna to return to Paris and to the prospect, now that a daughter had been born and survived, of very thin times. Perhaps journalism might be a straw to clutch at. Lenglet could write articles and if Jean translated them he/they might become a regular European correspondent for a Fleet Street paper. Jean Rhys began what networking of appropriate contacts might be possible. It was suggested she get in touch with Ford Madox Ford.

But now Lenglet's chickens had transmogrified into a cooked goose. The French authorities arrested him on a charge of embezzlement and, perhaps worse, for being resident in France when an illegal alien. He was sent to prison. Jean Rhys' cup of woe was filled three times full and brimming over.

This, immensely compressed, is the personal history that was to provide the material for all – yes, all, of Jean Rhys' subsequent novels and short stories. And it will be seen at once that being down and out in Paris and London was not the outcome of a sociological–literary experiment, however admirable, but the existential stuff of inescapable bloody life. She might well have gone to the wall there and then. But in her thrashing about to find some income, some occupation, some escape, she had followed up the suggestion that she contact Ford Madox Ford. In two differing but not unconnected ways he offered her not a straw to clutch at but a lifeline.

In the first place – it may, in fact, have been the second – and while Lenglet was still in gaol, Jean Rhys became Ford's mistress. This clearly happened with the tacit non-objection of Ford's long-term partner of that era, the Australian artist Stella Bowen. Bowen, under no illusion as to Ford's compulsively serial womanising, may well have preferred to have the current fling under partial control. (She may well have also fancied a bit of a rest.) Certainly this metaphorically laid back attitude granted Jean Rhys a roof over her head, hot food in her belly and some pocket money. It also put her cheek by jowl with the literary mentor her talent, latent to the point of invisibility, cried out for.

Amid a lifetime's plethora of very uneven writing, Ford produced two masterpieces. *The Good Soldier* and the *Parade's End* sequence are arguably the greatest novels written in English in the twentieth century. He was also a literary editor of genius. Twice, with the *English Review* in London before the Great War and now in Paris in the mid-1920s with the *transatlantic review*, he briefly presided over magazines of the greatest distinction. He had an amazing nose for recognising nascent ability. He gave starts or shop-windows to a score of relative unknowns who now inhabit the Pantheon of PhD theses. Lawrence, Arnold Bennett, Hemingway, Gertrude Stein, Picasso, Tristan Zsara, Dos Passos make up only a preliminary list of the talents to whom Ford offered opportunity and momentum.

Now he had more than just a sexual eye on Jean Rhys. He was encouraging her to write. And she was responding.

In 1924 the *transatlantic review* offered readers Jean Rhys' first published short story. *Vienne* was virtually as straight from life as a Stella Bowen portrait. From the same direct source other stories and snapshot sketches followed. The *transatlantic review* folded as inevitably as did the affair with its editor, but by now Jean Rhys was writing regularly. In 1927 Jonathan Cape published her first book – a collection of twenty-two of her stories brought out under the appropriate enough title (since it was hawked on the dust jacket as "sketches and studies of Bohemian Paris") as *The Left Bank*. It was Ford, still a name to be reckoned with in literary London, who had stepped forward as a genuinely honest broker to introduce his protégée to an English readership and he contributed an introduction to the collection.

He comments at one point on this newcomer's "terrifying instinct and a terrific – an almost lurid! – passion for stating the case of the underdog". Then, further into the introduction he writes: "When I, lately, edited a periodical, Miss Rhys sent in several communications with which I was immensely struck, and of which I published as many as I could. What struck me on the technical side was the singular instinct for form possessed by this young lady, an instinct for form being possessed by singularly few writers of English and by almost no English women writers."

"Lurid" and "form". As we shall see – for, dear readers, we shall come to *Wide Sargasso Sea* in time – Ford's literary perception was as accurate as ever.

The latest liaison was over; divorce proceedings shadowed the doomed marriage. But newly confident in the writing skills she had discovered she possessed Jean Rhys for a long decade was relatively self-possessed as well. She wrote and published four novels – *Quartet* (1928); *After Leaving Mr. Mackenzie* (1930); *Voyage in the Dark* (1934); *Good Morning, Midnight* (1939).

All four of these novels, in my opinion, are thoroughly admirable: but the last, obviously, was published on the eve of a war that not only swept millions away in death but consigned Jean Rhys to well-nigh total oblivion. Indeed she had disappeared from fashionable sight so completely that most literary and publishing contacts she had once known came to assume her dead as well. When, triumphantly, she emerged from nowhere in 1966 with *Wide Sargasso Sea*, her most substantial and significant work, it was not only to win golden opinions and literary prizes but, as well, to almost universal astonishment. As, able to pay her water rates again, she remarked: "It was tactless of me to be still alive on being rediscovered."

I have momentarily jumped ahead by a quarter of a century to make a point. Now that, in her late seventies, she had become a highly commercial 'property', the publishing industry which had for so long so egregiously neglected her returned to press about her. As a consequence a second collection of short stories *Sleep It Off Lady* was published in 1968 and then, posthumously, a sliver of quasi-autobiographical memoir *Smile, Please* (1979). She began this last in 1976 but her literary fastidiousness and her not unnatural desire to airbrush away many of the humiliating episodes in her past combined with the increasing infirmity of her remaining three years to prevent her progressing beyond, at best count, half-way. Nevertheless, wistfully graceful, *Smile, Please* provides some indication of how far, by her art, Jean Rhys was able to transcend the raw material of her life.

Sleep It Off Lady does her *oeuvre* a disservice. It lowers the overall tone. Its stories by and large are nothing much to write home about. But they have an interesting structure. Quite discrete in content, they are arranged chronologically – from childhood to death and, indeed, beyond. (It is the last two stories which redeem the collection.) My point is that exactly the same construction could be achieved in an amalgamation of Jean Rhys' first four novels. It would be relatively easy for a half-way competent hack to dovetail the four separate narratives into a single, seemingly seamless chronicle. There would be absolutely no advantage in doing this. On the contrary it would be insultingly deleterious. But I raise the ugly spectre to make as emphatically as possible the point that the four novels stretching from 1928 to 1939 are all variations on a theme if not, indeed, unvarying extensions of a theme.

2

The Narrow English Channel

Ford's satisfaction at having his judgement vindicated when his protégée published *Quartet* must have been severely qualified when he discovered the novel's content. *Quartet* we may irrelevantly say is a *roman à clef* ("Heidler is, of course, Ford." No, he's not. He's a character in a novel.) and the portrait for which he sat is not without its kiss-and-tell warts:

> He wasn't a good lover, of course. He didn't really like women. She had known that as soon as he touched her. His hands were inexpert, clumsy at caresses; his mouth was hard when he kissed …. He despised love. He thought of it grossly, to amuse himself, and then with furious contempt. Not that that mattered. He might be right. On the other hand, he might just possibly be wrong. But it didn't really matter much. What mattered was that, despising, almost disliking love, he was forcing her to be nothing but the little woman who loved in the Hōtel du Bosphore for the express purpose of being made love to. A *petite femme*.

But however great Ford's chagrin his *amour propre* would have been somewhat restored by a passage in the narrative downstream from the sad, sour analysis above:

> He whispered: 'Open your eyes, savage. Open your eyes, savage.' She opened her eyes and said: 'I love you, I love you, I love you. Oh please be nice to me. Oh, please say something nice to me I love you.' She was quivering and abject in his arms, like some unfortunate dog abasing itself before its master.

This is significant. We do not have to be too versed in all things Freudian to recognise that all Jean Rhys' "abject" protagonists share in common with their creator the need for a father figure. In her fragment of memoir Rhys makes very clear her affection for her father. His death within some three years of her taking what they both would have thought was temporary leave of each other, a death occurring when, not yet twenty, she was three thousand miles or more apart from him can only have hit her lastingly hard. Seventy years later, close to her own end, she flatly recorded it. 'It still seems strange to me that he's dead.' When, a decade later she married Lenglet there would have been the illusion of security in his 'take-charge' chancer's nerve. After their divorce she eventually married her literary agent in London and then, on his relatively early death, his cousin. Neither of these marriages, at a distance, smack highly of Romantic Love.

It is left unspoken, but certainly for Marya, the victim-heroine of *Quartet*, certainly for her counterparts in the three other novels of the 1930s, the downward spiral is in part an (inevitably futile) search for something more than a chic dress on their backs, a roof over their heads and a pillow, shared or not, on which to lay their heads. As Anita Loos, an interestingly parallel life, might have told each one of them, it is the second noun in the expression 'sugar daddy' that carries the greater resonance.

Quartet received its finally settled title from the American publishers who rightly took exception to its being originally called *Postures* in a too pretentiously oblique attempt to signal the masquerading attitudes of its protagonists. But *Quartet* itself is not so entirely apt. It aims to indicate the *pas de quatre* of the two married couples. But although the novel employs a third-person narrative it is from the viewpoint of Marya that the story is over-whelmingly told. As is the case with her sisters under the skin – Anna in *Voyage in the Dark*, Julia in *After Leaving Mr. Mackenzie*, Sasha in *Good Morning, Midnight* (that other 'quartet' whose lives might be made a continuous narrative) – it is Marya's darkening progress along her Parisian *via dolorosa* that rivets us. Ford may well have found fault with the somewhat crude recourse to melodrama – only partially redeemed by a nicely rancid, ironic coda – with which Rhys, still a relative tyro, untypically concludes *Quartet*. But his own ruffled feathers once back in place, he would have had the literary discrimination to admire the withering objectivity with which Rhys charts the route. 'Lurid' was his word in introducing her to the public. Writing in an era when fully frontal nudity on prime-time television is routine, I would rather opt, I believe, for 'steely' or 'uncompromisingly dark'.

The 'sister' protagonists of Rhys' first four novels confront the world without resource. Their early prettiness has been their downfall. They have been 'ruined' in more than the sense of the Victorian euphemism. As the narrator of the early short story *Vienne* levelly acknowledges: "Men have spoilt me – always disdaining my mind and concentrating on my body."

For they do have minds. They have intelligence and sensibilities. Too much so. They are incapable of trudging their way through life as chamber-maids or laundresses. They have been spoilt in that sense too. The same young wife in Vienna had stated: "I knew that I could never be poor again with courage or dignity." But just as she, each of the dubious heroines of the novels does find herself poor: finds herself alone, adrift and without a penny or *sou* to her name. Each finds herself without either the skill that would offer her a livelihood and provide an armature for her existence or a man able to proffer much the same benefits. The consequent downward spiral is inevitable.

Rhys presents the respective banal, enormous calamities with a flat objectivity. Having been here herself, she knows these landscapes of city and mind. She recreates them with a chilling authenticity.

Both in terms of narrative sequence and of syntax the literary form that imparts such a quasi-documentary impression is parataxis. That is to say: this happens and then this happens and then that happens and this happens. It is the perfectly judged mode for these lost souls, as, belonging nowhere and to no one, they move from pillar to post – the mean back streets, the shoddy restaurant, the dingy lodgings – as living from hand to mouth, they find their lives reduced to a constant present of one thing happening after another. They endeavour (never with anaesthetising success) to forget the past: remembered happinesses or disasters are now both alike too painful to recall. And because they do not have one they cannot, they dare not, think about the future. The thing is to just get through this day, this evening, this moment. My moment. Overwhelmingly, whether the narrative is in the first or third person, we experience the moment from the viewpoint of the sufferer. This example from *After Leaving Mr. Mackenzie* is typical in its effortless blending of exterior and interior observation:

> Julia thought: 'They might light the street a bit better, here.'
>
> It was the darkness that got you. It was heavy darkness, greasy and compelling. It made walls round you, and shut you in so that you felt you could not breathe. You wanted to beat at the darkness and shriek to be let out. And after a while you got used to it. Of course. And then you stopped believing that there was anything else anywhere.
>
> The singer – a drably vague figure standing as near as he dared to the entrance to a public bar – had started *The Pagan Love Song* for the second time.
>
> The buses would stop near the pub. She got on the next one that was going in the direction of Oxford Circus, mounted to the top, and sat there with her eyes shut.

There is a precision of vision and experience here. There is an economy of means in conveying them.

I shall forgo insulting Jean Rhys, the reader and myself by labelling her a 'Modernist' – that fashionable categorisation that virtually no academic can define with any precision approaching utility. It is sufficient for present purposes to say that Jean Rhys was a writer with her own voice and of her own time, and that time was post-World War One and Henry James had died in 1916. More pertinently, I would point up that Jean Rhys in Paris in the 1920s found herself cheek by distant jowl – in a late, surviving letter she talks of "knowing him not personally but by sight" – both in the *transatlantic review*'s portfolio of emerging talent and in Montparnasse *boîtes* with the nine-years younger Ernest Hemingway.

Hemingway may have been by so much her junior, but his very first novel anticipated Rhys' by a year. I cannot but believe that, perhaps, even in 'work in progress' stage, Hemingway's *The Sun Also Rises* influenced *Quartet*. After all on that tedious *roman à clef* level ("Cairn, of course, is really Ernest Hemingway." "No, he's not. He's Ivan Brede." No, both wrong, Cairn is a character in a novel) the American appears in *Quartet* in a supporting role.

One of the most attractive features of *The Sun Also Rises* is the manner in which Hemingway deploys the city of Paris as an ever-present, ever-changing background to his narrative – a moveable feast for his characters. The City of Light vibrates positively the better to darken the Lost Generation's three-in-the-morning *angst*. Jean Rhys uses much the same trick and arguably to better effect. The background Paris we see out of the corner of her protagonists' eyes is meanly and darkly in tune with their ill fortune. It is those meaner side and back streets that she has them walk – less because they are going anywhere than because when down and out in Paris walking is something to do to pass the time.

Hemingway, heir to the Sawyeresque hints Mark Twain bequeathed him, is, of course, the cliché exemplar of minimalist, 'unliterary' narrative prose. But Rhys to a large degree walked in his footsteps. If her heroine victims are soft-centred her prose inclines to the hard-boiled. It is the called-for style. Since, to repeat, the protagonists go down their *via dolorosa* in a perpetual present – that unremitting succession of one thing after another – it is entirely appropriate to record the sequence in short, sharp 'this happened and then this happened' paratactic prose. But to do so courts a very considerable danger. Although pulverising in their impact upon Rhys' lost souls, the insults that circumstance inflicts upon them are in the greater scheme of things prosaic. It is, of course, the essence of the personal tragedies that they are 'banal' but to unfold a lengthening list of seemingly small-scale happenings in even, pared-down sentences would seem to risk going beyond a documentary realism into the realms of boredom. It is a major accomplishment of Jean Rhys' art that almost invariably she avoids this pitfall.

To begin with, other than in her dialogue (where they serve to help define the speaker's character) her prose is devoid of clichés. Her descriptions embellish the everyday with a freshness which makes us see it as if for the first time. This ability stems in part from her not wearing so altogether strident a 'tough-guy prose stylist' badge on her literary sleeve. She is not afraid to seek out subtle effects. In the example cited above, for instance, she describes the street singer as cutting a 'drably vague figure'. Modest though it seems, the coupling of that adverb and that adjective strikes me as a juxtaposition of an appropriate subtlety not so many novelists have looked to achieve. The phrase approaches the poetic in its compression and, like another contemporary, Dawn Powell, Jean Rhys occasionally allows the poet in her close to full expression. This is the reflection of Anna Morgan, the protagonist of *Voyage in the Dark*, when at best part-drunk and totally desperate:

> It was one of those days when you can see the ghosts of all the
> other lovely days. You drink a bit and watch the ghosts of all the
> lovely days that have ever been from behind a glass.

The words and syntax are simple. But the repetition, the buried pun and, above all, the (author's) perception entirely banish the remotest thought of tedium. This is how Sappho might have written if she had been born on her island in 1890.

This short quotation also demonstrates another factor which constantly refreshes Jean Rhys' prose. She had the most wonderful ear – word by word, sentence upon sentence, paragraph after paragraph – for cadence. This is a quality not readily to be illustrated by short extracts, but, reverting again to the 'street singer' example above, let me cite the flat, accumulative, perfect rhythm with which it concludes.

Jean Rhys laboured hard, it is recorded, at shaping and polishing her prose. She constantly rewrote her rewritings. This characteristic is one of two she shares with another contemporary writer, Raymond Chandler, just two years her senior. Both write prose which for immediate purposes we might describe in crude shorthand as 'hard-boiled literary'. And both are writers who progressed to the novel from short stories by extensively revisiting their earlier work to cannibalise. *Quartet*, to cite a very obvious example, recycles the *Left Bank*'s dour, documentary account of a Visitors' Day encounter of young wife with imprisoned husband.

Rhys and Chandler were both living in England before the Great War. One is driven to speculate. Did that fit-up version of *Our Miss Gibbs* ever tour as far south as Lewisham? Was there a rainy Thursday night when, for want of a better alternative, Chandler dropped in at the theatre? Did their eyes lock across the footlights? If so, if he had then danced his stage-door attendance upon her what a loss in reading pleasure might have been inflicted upon millions by their complete fulfilment in each other's company ... But *revenons* ...

Just as the subtly structured cadences of her narrative passages demonstrate the sensitivity of Jean Rhys' ear, so too her dialogue shows its acuteness. When she sets her characters to talk she writes splendid dialogue. It does not give us the self-conscious, exchanges – "look, I'm making literature out of common-or-garden demotic" – of Pinter or of Hemingway lapsing into self-parody. Her dialogue sounds utterly natural but, carefully wrought, it is multi-functional. It further defines or qualifies character and relationships. It advances the plot, complicates situations. It implies variations on the novels' grim underlying themes. Here is a brief conversational exchange between Julia Martin in *After Leaving Mr. Mackenzie* and George Horsfield the Englishman, neither young nor old, whom she has blundered into hard upon executing the novel's title. In essence he is her male counterpart – irresolute, unfulfilled, lacking direction. Through the sad inevitability of mutual default they will become bedfellows. But Horsfield is crucially different from Julia in one respect. He has money. They talk as they come to the end of yet another of the countless meals she has had men buy for her:

> She realized with a shock that the meal was nearly over. She thought: 'If I'm going to do it at all I must do it now.' She felt nervous and shivered. 'I'm awfully cold,' she said.
>
> It was stupid that, when you had done this sort of thing a hundred times, you still felt nervous and shivered as you were doing it.
>
> Mr Horsfield stared at her and said: 'What's the matter? Are things going badly?' He thought: 'After all, fifteen hundred francs isn't much. Fancy having to rely for good and all on fifteen hundred francs!' And then he thought: 'Oh, God, I hope she isn't going to cry.'
>
> He said: 'Look here, let's go somewhere else and talk. Don't tell me about things here. We'll go somewhere else to talk.'
>
> She said speaking quickly: 'You surprised me, because people nearly always force you to ask, don't they?'
>
> 'They do,' said Mr Horsfield.

Her face was red. She went on talking in an angry voice: 'They force you to ask – and then they refuse you. And then they tell you all about why they refuse you. I suppose they get a subtle pleasure out of it, or something.'

Mr Horsfield said: 'Subtle pleasure? Not at all. A very simple and primitive pleasure.'

'It's so easy to make a person who hasn't got anything seem wrong.'

'Yes,' he said. 'I know. That's dawned on me once or twice, extraordinary as it may seem. It's always so damned easy to despise hard-up people when in one way and another you're as safe as houses. Have another liqueur.'

But he was relieved when she declined, because he was afraid she looked rather drunk. He watched her anxiously, feeling at once very intimate with her. And he hated the feeling of intimacy. It made something in him shrink back and long to escape.

She made her inevitable, absent-minded gesture of powdering her face. She looked happier and relieved. That, of course, was because she imagined that she was now going to cast all her woes on his shoulders. Which was all very well, he thought, but he had his own troubles.

There is a fleck of Conrad about this exchange. Two empty lives with their agendas askew are going to fail to coalesce. We can be sure of this because of the ease with which Jean Rhys skips across the table to sit in Horsfield's seat. Her novels overwhelmingly unfold from her victim-heroine's point of view. But not exclusively so. As and when occasion demands she effortlessly inhabits the thought processes and inner language of subsidiary characters. As will shortly be newly evident, the facility with which she could shift viewpoints is a prime strength of her fifth, last and finest novel.

It is as much by the acuity of her vision as her subtle prose rhythms that Jean Rhys avoids the danger of tedium potentially lurking in flat 'one thing after another' story-telling. The colours of her cityscapes are muted. They are nevertheless vivid. Telling details, carefully chosen, fix locations and ambiences sharply in our minds. She describes with that immediacy of impression that her heroines, living in their hand-to-mouth present, have to be alive to if they are not to go under. Julia Martin and her sister-victims ceaselessly scan the immediate world about them. They know they need to be on the constant *qui vive* to detect – that is the word – the insincerity in that welcoming smile, the enmity covert in the conventional greeting, the imminent betrayal in the lover's kiss. This outlook of the vulnerable and broken upon the world which cruelly confronts them was once their creator's own. This is terrain she traversed herself; territory she has personally researched. It gives her tremendous literary advantage. Remembering, she knows precisely which are the handful of details she needs to provide to give token completion to the current scene. At the outset of *After Leaving Mr. Mackenzie*, for example, she describes a rented room:

> Julia paid sixteen francs a night. Her room on the second floor was large and high-ceilinged, but it had a sombre and one-eyed aspect because the solitary window was very much to one side.

By the standards of many a Rhys room this one is comparatively salubrious. But even as we visualise it for ourselves we know no good will ensue from a stay here. More than the window will be out of kilter. And this is absolutely typical. Realistic as her descriptions at first-glance, surface level almost invariably are, many of them also vibrate with a subtextual poetic resonance that, until we pause to take a second glance, works on an unconscious level. Thus she writes:

> The restaurant was long and narrow. Red-shaded lamps stood on the tables, and the walls were decorated with paintings of dead birds served up on plates ready to be eaten, with flowers and piles of fruit in gilt baskets.

As readers we do not make a meal of this scene-setting description but something within us knows that little good will come to people choosing to dine in a place like this.

Since sharpness of ear and eye allied to an achieved – because worked-at and won – ability to put appropriate words down on the page in the best of orders allows Jean Rhys to write poetically leavened, laconic prose and set scenes with a matching economy, her novels are brief as to length and graced with momentum. But these qualities combine to produce perhaps Jean Rhys' first four novels' most impressive virtue – the objectivity with which they are presented.

Ford Madox Ford once concurred with Joseph Conrad that when Maupassant wrote of a character, 'He was a gentleman with red whiskers who always went first through a doorway,' he had told us all we needed to know about how the man would subsequently behave. Over yet another *fine* Ford must have (yet again) repeated the exchange to Rhys.

To return at last to the oblique entry point of this study, I would highlight the fact that there is no 'editorialising' in Jean Rhys' work. She does not, as author, presume to tell us what to think. Encounters, exchanges are not subjected to first-person analysis. Downtrodden, ill-used, their own worst enemies as they are, her heroine-victims do not complain or repine. They do not buttonhole the reader with 'The world owes me a living!'

Yes, in the bleakest of all *Good Morning, Midnight*, Sasha Jensen may say: 'A room is a place where you hide from the wolves outside.' She may say to the sadly off-beam gigolo: 'I'm no use to anybody. I'm a *cérébrale*, can't you see that?' But these are not complaints. Whether to another or herself these are grim, deadpan acknowledgements of what she perceives to be the unvarnished truth. Given the spiritual defeats and humiliations they have undergone, Jean Rhys' characters are remarkably acceptant of their fate. Even when knowing in their heart of hearts that midnight is already upon them and that the efforts they are still making to arrest their downwards spiral are no more than token, they still appear remarkably stoic. This is what they've come to deserve. Like Sasha Jensen, they will have to accept what they can get. A *cérébrale*, too clever by half, nowhere near clever enough … no real complaints, then …

The reader is left to infer. We are left to deduce the grief, the fear, the sense of loss, the hunger, humiliation and shame ourselves. Jean Rhys makes unerringly sure that we do.

It is the very austerity of her constantly objective presentation which brings out the best in us as readers With the occasional stimuli of choice visual details that imply an entire setting or conjure a mood, she deploys her beautifully rhythmed 'unliterary' prose to confront us with vignette after framed vignette that *we* must interpret. Such tact. Intimate familiarity with her subject matter does not breed complacency. Because she herself was once there she does not permit detail or description to blur because this smudged reference has instant resonance – it happened to her and was important – to her. Nor does she surrender to quasi-autobiography. She does not permit herself that first-person spoon-feeding by which Proust and Powell and more latterly, however adroitly, John Banville, signpost to their readers how they should think. Although steeped in the milieu of her settings, Jean Rhys, as novelist, was able to disengage her talent the better to work at recreating them.

The somewhat cheap gibe that by uniting the heroines of Jean Rhys' first four novels into a progressively ageing, single protagonist one could carpenter an omnibus serial is not without a grain of justification. To read all four in quick succession is to induce in one's head the same sort of disorientation that drinking four glasses of the heroines' tipple of choice, Pernod *fils*, brings on. The novels are variations on a theme – and not such varying variations at that. Their structures are essentially identical. The furrow they plough is narrow.

They are anecdotes drawn from a tiny section of the human condition rather than magisterial overviews. They do not vouchsafe us new revelations about the Human Condition, Man's dubious position in the universal scheme of things. Rather the pre-World War Two work of Jean Rhys serves to remind us of the sad truths to be found just beyond our current comfort zones. "Yes," we say because she has led us in effect to experience them, "this is how it happens."

For this reason I do not think that any of the four novels may be called masterpieces. They are simply too slight – too slight when put alongside the fifteen or so masterpiece novels that have been written in the past two centuries.

But judged as the minor-key works they do not pretend to be other than, it has to be said that, largely, the four novels hit their target squarely in the centre. That is their success: that is their kind of perfection.

Thus it is, I believe, we do emerge from reading them enlightened and enhanced. For all but a very few of us, it is devoutly to be wished, the world, the circumstances, the victimised souls they depict come as eye-openers or, at worst, reminders. And in so far as – on that lowest level, at least – we come away from a reading thinking 'There but for the grace of God,' Jean Rhys' novels do enhance us. Not only do they acquaint us with, or remind us of the predatory and selfish in the world they choose to evoke, but, along with admiration for their achieved artistry, they evoke our compassion for that same world's dispossessed.

3

The Wide Sargasso Sea

It is fascinating to learn (from a surviving letter written as late as 1966) that Jean Rhys first read Charlotte Brontë's *Jane Eyre* when she was between sixteen and seventeen years old – "a very impressionable age". It was later, then, than that time when, as *Smile, Please* describes, child rather than adolescent, she first sought the bookworm's refuge from the pressures and tedium of the immediate world about her:

> There was the usual glassed-in bookcase at the end of the sitting room … I can still see … several history books, yellow-backed novels and on the top shelf a rather odd selection of poets, Milton, Byron, then Crabbe, Cowper, Mrs. Hemans, also *Robinson Crusoe, Treasure Island, Gulliver's Travels, Pilgrim's Progress.*

Later, still in Roseau, in the Victoria Memorial Library, a novel of prophetic import caught the growing girl's increasingly roving eye:

> No one ever advised me what to read or forbade me to read something … I liked books about prostitutes, there were a good many then, and vividly recollect a novel called *The Sands of Pleasure* written by a man named Filson Young. It must have been well written otherwise I would never have remembered it so perfectly to this day. It was about an Englishman's love affair with an expensive demi-mondaine in Paris.

Another volume that had earlier come into the escapist reader's hands was a bowdlerised version of the *Arabian Nights*. This is a title Jean Rhys salutes sixty years later in 'The Day they Burnt the Books'. In this short story, wherein she characteristically projects elements of her own recollected experience into the solidity of impersonal fiction, an incipiently literate young girl is given access to the Aladdin's cave of his father's well-stocked library through the good offices of a friend. The time and place are those of Rhys' own Dominican childhood. Significantly her friend's mother is a mulatto: in his frequent cups her white, English husband is given to insulting her in the grossest racial manner. On his dying, the widow burns his books. The years of humiliation have stoked up a hatred which has passed into the vengefully irrational. This premise had historical precedent. Whether they were married or spinster, Dominica was home to a distinct bevy of inbred, irrational women. One such was a beautiful Creole girl who, on securing a proposal from a wealthy young English visitor to the island, showed her engagement ring to the whole world. Then, leaving her at the altar, so to speak, he had overnight fled the island aboard the Royal Mail. The jilted girl's violent and obscene reaction to the disgrace she believed that she had endured was merely the prelude to a life of semi-catatonic rejection of everything about her. It was a 'sister's' fate Ella Gwen Williams well remembered into her Jean Rhys days.

It may have been as a teenager in Cambridge in 1906 or 1907 that she first read *Jane Eyre*, but the moment did not come there. It did not come in a focused inspiration for half a century. Yet a moment certainly did come – in 1957 to be precise – as we know from a letter written the next year that talks of 'it clicking in my head'. It must have been a golden moment, in very truth, when adrenalin flashed right the way through her as in that flash she thought: 'I have it!' For a second her mind would have leapt forward to the end of the long, tortuous, torturing process and she would have seen the book she had just – but at last! – conceived complete and out upon the world.

Perhaps, misled by the 1958 letter – Jean Rhys is the ultimately ambiguous purveyor of reminiscences – I romanticise. As early as the 1930 published *After Leaving Mr. Mackenzie* she has her heroine speak of a 'friend' who in every totally vulnerable mistress' fantasy indulges in the wishful thinking that her lover will go blind and that at a stroke their roles will be reversed. Carole Angier (see Bibliography below) affirms that in 1945 she had 'half finished' a 'Mrs Rochester' novel. The build-up to the illuminating flash may have occupied more than a decade. And yet I persist: surely there is a poetic truth in imagining a magical moment when, with crystal vision, Jean Rhys saw that what for Charlotte Brontë was no more than a mechanical plot contrivance was her own story writ Gothic and small. Yes, and now she would redress the balance. She would write her own version large!

Since I believe, dear reader, that neither you nor I are academics concerned to outwit or manoeuvre colleagues in the battle for superior tenure, let us have no truck here with concepts such as re- or deconstruction. Jean Rhys simply saw in that moment when it clicked in her head that she could thrust her hand into the core of *Jane Eyre* and, as if the novel were a sock, pull it inside out. She would take the contrivance – the former Bertha Mason, a deranged Creole immured in a cold English attic because, out of her mind, she must needs be out of sight and, *voilà!* – make her the centrepiece protagonist of, if not a riposte, a politically corrected alternative to *Jane Eyre.*

The earlier novel was published in 1847. For its first readers the setting was contemporary. For Jean Rhys, graced by her inspired insight over a century later, the need was to write a historical novel. Yet in the reading *Wide Sargasso Sea* is not a historical novel at all. It is its psychological intensity and the universality of the extreme emotions it discloses that compel. We are not at all drawn into the narrative by those evocations of former ages, subtle and entirely relevant though they may be, which we occasionally find in such 'historical' novels as *Vanity Fair* or *War and Peace.* The Dominica of Jean Rhys' childhood in the 1890s would have altered scarcely at all either in appearance or ambience over the previous six decades. Although in other respects the setting is crucially important to her purpose, she has not the slightest interest in penning a retrospective travelogue or a literary waxwork. To move the action from the West Indies to the North of England did not require, she considered, a four page bravura description of a windjammer beating its way across the Atlantic. Sketched in sufficiently to give us our bearings, the settings on an immediate level are merely background. They are simply there and essentially timeless. At key moments, of course, Jean Rhys puts them to far more subtle use. But nothing is given houseroom in the novel simply because it is picturesque or quaint.

In this regard let us blow one misconception out of the water once and for all. *Wide Sargasso Sea* is a serious novel in conception and execution entirely in its own right. It is not a pastiche. It is not, least of all, ever to be linked to that unspeakably distasteful species of conclusions to the likes of *Sanditon* or *The Mystery of Edwin Drood.* It is an original work.

But if Jean Rhys did not see her excursion back to the past as reason to swash a historical buckle, we might have nevertheless have imagined that the change in period would possibly have called forth from her – especially as she approached her own old age – a looser, more discursive prose style. We might have anticipated longer sentences, a greater use of dependent clauses. This is not the case. The background is often exotic and the states of mind often extreme, but they do not give rise to unworthily self-conscious 'fine' writing. The sentences continue brief and to the point. Monosyllables their norm they record things that, one after another, happen or have happened. They recount the softer-edged memories that foreground events reconjure. *Plus ça change* in this respect. The prose, the occasional recourse to time-shift, are in essence the same that Rhys employed in taking her crippled heroines through the Paris and London of the 1920s and 1930s. For good immediate reason: Antoinette

Cosway, her genuinely tragic heroine now, is Marya, Julia, Anna and Sasha driven to the extreme.

Wide Sargasso Sea contains enough matter, of course, to call forth from another sensibility a three-decker Victorian novel even longer than *Jane Eyre*. That Jean Rhys arrives at her conclusion in so much shorter a compass is due in part to her spare prose. In the first page of *Wild Sargasso Sea* she gives us a suicide and the malevolent poisoning of a horse – two incidents which in 'for want of a nail' fashion impact directly upon subsequent events. The suicide is over and done with in a sentence:

> One calm evening he shot his dog, swam out to sea and was gone for always.

The consequence is stated in a laconic paragraph:

> Mr. Lutrell's house was left empty, shutters banging in the wind. Soon the black people said it was haunted, they wouldn't go near it. And no one came near us.

The economy, let us be sure, is not merely a matter of not being verbose. The long hiatus since her last novel had not robbed Jean Rhys of her touch of poetry. When she has need she is able to deploy the poet's gift of compression, of being able to speak volumes in a sentence. In the recounting above of the suicide, the seemingly unnecessary word 'calm' works a subliminal wonder in setting the ironic scene. Similarly, not much further into the narrative Antoinette recalls returning home as a child after suffering a shattering betrayal that has left her, she feels, like something not even the cat would drag in. Elegant ladies and gentlemen attending a soirée spy her and redouble the humiliation. Antoinette remembers running into a bedroom where

> I stood with my back against the door and I could feel my heart all through me.

The second half of that sentence (not spectacularly inventive, all but one word a monosyllable) has a freshness and directness that arrest us and convey the experience – a fictional commonplace, be it noted – with mint-new impact. It knocks our own heart. Proust would have wrung some 30 pages out of that 'moment' against the door. He would not have bettered the effect.

This is crucial to an appreciation of Jean Rhys. What overwhelmingly lends her narrative its economy of effort and its rapidity of momentum is her continued confidence in – or disregard for! – her reader. She continues to have faith enough to imply and not explain. She is willing to back her ability to interest her readers into entering into her text and meeting her half-way. On an equal footing. She does not lazily pile up adjectives, tell the reader what she has just implied. There is never a cliché either of word or thought. She revisits each experience or impression, no matter how commonplace, as if – miraculously – for the first time and, recreating it on the page, makes it fresh for us.

Here is an almost sublime example of Jean Rhys' ability to revivify the commonplace by imbuing it with the feeling that this immediate example is the original *aperçu*. At the start of the novel's second section Antoinette and Rochester (never once, of course, so coarsely labelled) are on their way to Grandbois, their ill-fated honeymoon retreat. By virtue of its conception *Wide Sargasso Sea* is in no way a novel of suspense – we rather think we know that there will be tears before bedtime – and Rhys here wants to increase the sense of foreboding Rochester must endure. In two or three sentences she establishes that the couple have been forced to shelter from heavy rain close to a beach. There she has Rochester observe:

> The rain fell more heavily, huge drops sounded like hail on the leaves of the tree, and the sea crept stealthily forwards and backwards.

The first half of the sentence *is* a commonplace. But it is there to set up what follows. That image! That choice of the word 'stealthily'! I wonder if anyone else ever, Homer included, has looked at the sea ebbing to and fro upon a beach and conjured quite so quietly ominous an effect. The tone is anything but Homeric but the precision the of draw-your-own-conclusion is of a quality he would be happy to acknowledge as his own.

The misgivings that Rochester conveys as he stands next to his bride of a few hours and stares at the stealthily ominous sea are not misplaced. He has married in bad faith. He has reason to feel uneasy. In *Jane Eyre* this union is, to repeat, nothing but a plotting device. Its function is to make Rochester inaccessible: forbidden father-figure fruit. Thanks to it Charlotte Brontë can put heroine and virgin reader through a series of bemused hoops that include indulging everyone in the *frisson* of an interrupted wedding ceremony ("The marriage cannot go on: I declare the existence of an impediment"). But though the whole plot of her novel hangs upon it, Charlotte Brontë must needs skip over the circumstances of Rochester's marriage to Bertha Mason as fudgingly as plausible. He appears such a callow idiot else. As indeed he was. That is the *sine qua non* point. But to dwell upon his witless stupidity is to exclude him for ever from attaining the level of *gravitas* which is also essential to her story. If Rochester is to appear not only a sadder but a far wiser man in his middle age he cannot start from too low a level of intelligence.

Jean Rhys does rather better with this problem. To begin with borrowing (typically) from her father's own experience on first arrival in Dominica, she visits upon her Rochester an onset of the fever that she knew all about but of which Charlotte Brontë would have been thoroughly ignorant. So, contracting his marriage hard on the heels of his disease, Rhys' Rochester is not himself. As contrivances go, this is still thin. But a more satisfyingly plausible explanation of the decision to marry in haste underwrites the plot-serving device. Rochester agrees to take the hand of this intriguing and beautiful girl in this exotic place she somehow embodies in a fit of cynical pique. He is well aware that his father and elder brother (both of whom care no more for him than he has come to care for them) are conniving to bring about this alliance of potential nuisance (penniless younger son) with fiscal salvation (a hugely wealthy West Indian heiress). So be it, then! He will take the money and ridding himself of tawdry dependence upon them let the devil take the consequence. This is a tragic error but not entirely callow. And, on reflection, we come to understand from his attitude that, just as Antoinette Cosway, Rochester has also always lacked the benefit of a supportive family.

We are vouchsafed the outward circumstances of the marriage from Rochester's own lips. The central and longest section of *Wild Sargasso Sea* – and also the most difficult in the writing: Rhys tried on many versions for size – was finally cast in his first-person narration. Here again, having begun her novel in Antoinette's voice Jean Rhys is commendably chaste. Even as she did not sink to fustian 'historical' descriptions neither does she attempt here a bravura display of 'masculine' utterance. Totally without crude, external stage direction – Rhys continues to credit her readers with the intelligence to infer – the prose continues with only the subtlest of stylistic variations. There is no roistering Regency rake 'stap me vitals' nonsense. The sentences follow one on the other fractionally sharper, perhaps, than were Antoinette's; their rhythm is perhaps more staccato. But, as by the novel's conclusion Rochester gains a reputation among all around him as a cold, hard man, it is more from his observations and attitudes than the way in which he expresses them. We are led to conclude, more subliminally than not, that in terms of their respective intellects and abilities to verbalise Mr. and Mrs. Rochester are, or rather would have been, excellently matched.

To a tragic degree, however, no good does come of the marriage. Watching that sea wash in and out, Rochester already senses this outcome. All about him, his new bride most of all, is alien.

In her earlier – though twentieth-century – novels Jean Rhys uses the West Indies as a positive element. As she did herself, most of her benighted heroines have memories of the Caribbean – fond memories. As now, lost and directionless they wander the down-and-out streets of Paris and London those memories sometimes flicker vibrantly into life at the edge of their mental vision. The warmth and colour of those childhood scenes serve cruelly to make worse the drabness and above all the cold of the diminished present and the inevitable future. Dominica is a positive force. It is not so in *Wide Sargasso Sea*.

Since Charlotte Brontë set the original scene of Rochester's marriage in Spanish Town the main action of the later novel is nominally played out in an inherited Jamaica. But Jean Rhys was from another island – one still as vivid in her memory in her later years as it had been the day she left it. Topography was not to her purpose. She no more 'did' Jamaica than she chose to depict windjammers. Rather, she evokes a fuzzily defined isle that is full of noises that are not sweet and airs that are baneful and, at every turn, undercurrents positively noxious. The setting of *Wide Sargasso Sea* is the dark side of that mephitic Dominica which part of her had never left.

She does the ominous land- and sea scapes of this Dominica-Jamaica quite superbly. As always, even though the flora might encourage otherwise, her prose never becomes purple. It remains deft and economical. Yet nevertheless images she conjures are worthy of a Gaugin or a Douanier Rousseau. This is a sun-saturated, deep-shadowed tropical Eden. But it is an Eden where the apple has long since been eaten and snakes are on the loose. It is an Eden laid claim to by more than the one God of Antoinette's convent upbringing. And this obvious much Rochester knows. He knows ... but cannot decipher the aliennesses further. He is, he knows, like a man walking on the crust of a volcano all the time expecting it to give way. He can never be at home here.

Yet, despite being born and brought up here, neither can Antoinette Cosway. Hers is a still more pernicious alienation. Her hostile environment is not topographical but existential. In all this lush, exotic landscape there is nothing solid under her feet either.

Neither completely white nor black the family cannot continue to pay its social way. Worse, Antoinette's mother, pulverised less by widowhood than by unassailable grief that the son – upon whom, to her daughter's extreme detriment, she dotes – has been born an imbecile, is sunk into a half-catatonic stupor. Eating salt fish because they cannot afford fresh, the family lives raggedly on the poverty line and there only through the hand-to-mouth shifts of their impressively enigmatic housekeeper-cook – a woman whose bedroom presents to view not only the Catholic prayer for a happy death but, as well, in a corner, a heap of chicken feathers.

In their social limbo the Cosways are scorned by everyone. The colonial whites, regarding them as not the genuine article, ostracise them. To the blacks they are 'white cockroaches' – despised and hated with an open contempt. Antoinette's betraying black childhood friend puts their position succinctly:

> Plenty white people in Jamaica. Real white people, they got money. They didn't look at us, nobody see them come near us. Old time white people nothing but white nigger now, and black nigger better than white nigger.

Swaggering – but aimlessly so – the negroes seem an extension of the hostile landscape. Rhys conveys their sinister 'otherness' superbly, principally by evoking their 'patois':

> 'Listen, *doudou ché*. Plenty people fasten bad words on you and on your mother. I know it. I know who is talking and what they say. The man is not a bad man, even if he love money, but he hear so many stories he don't know what to believe. That is why he keep away. I put no trust in none of those people round you.'

Rhys' aural memory of when she first heard speech rhythms such as these in her own native Dominica seems perfect. Whether they are truly authentic for the year 1839 is now beyond collective memory to determine: but whether read in twenty-first-century London today or in Haworth Rectory that same second year of Victoria's reign, they must be adjudged to be entirely convincing.

The juxtaposition of Catholic prayer and chicken feathers in Christophine's bedroom is not random set-dressing. At the centre of Antoinette's young life, her dysfunctional home is a vacuum that, depriving her of an authority figure, denies her as well the possibility of gaining self-esteem. But wrapped around this vacuum are two influences that loom over her sensibility. It is not so central to Rhys' overall design as it is to Jacques Tourneur in his own commendable extension of *Jane Eyre*, his *I Walked with a Zombie*, but from the jungle and the island's black inhabitants, sinisterly and convincingly, comes *obeah*. In the convent that Antoinette comes to attend is Catholicism. Both of these belief systems are canted strongly towards the contemplation and even celebration of death: both, so to speak, mark Antoinette for life. In that brief period when she and her husband are able to 'magic' each other and sexual fulfilment seems to be bringing happiness she says to him:

'If I could die now. Now, when I am happy ... Say die and I will die. You don't believe me? Then try, say die and watch me die.'

As readers we may doubt that the intensity of the two super-ego belief systems could be so immediately final. But we do not doubt the sincerity of Antoinette's own belief. Very early in her life she had made a terrible observation:

'I know the time of day when though it is hot and blue and there are no clouds, the sky can have a very black look.'

She has since learnt that there are worse things in life than death.

Antoinette comes to study at the convent because, miraculously, her mother's beauty wins her a second husband. It is a match that sets a precedent. Mr Mason (as Antoinette will always think of him: he is not a father-figure) is white and rich and blind to his environment. He does not bring salvation but only a dubious and temporary respite. White 'society', it is true, is now obliged to recognise the reconstituted family. But the blacks, so vehement before as they looked down on the 'white cockroach' Conways from below, can only take to hating them, in their restored prosperity with redoubled force. Emancipation has given the until recently exploited slaves freedom but not occupation: making work for idle hands, the devil supplies the want. Incensed by talk of the imminent importation of 'coolie' labour into their island, the blacks become an unstructured mob and burn Antoinette's newly refurbished but ill-starred home to the ground. The financial loss is but a trifle now. But the incident precipitate's Antoinette's descent into authentic tragedy.

Since some of the house servants are involved, the firing of the house is freighted with a sad betrayal. But, immediately, it is in the physical doing that it is most frighteningly harmful. It accelerates a death. Although Antoinette's mother hurtles through flames to rescue her idiot son from his blazing bedroom he is dead before the night is out. The loss permanently crazes the mother's senses. Soon, nominally for her own good (out of mind, best out of sight), she has been shut away and made subject to, possibly complicit in, the most gross obviousnesses of abuse. As Antoinette discovers. Her compassionate but childishly ill-judged attempts to visit the mother she so resembles in appearance – they share, Jean Rhys delicately indicates, the same vertical crease in their foreheads – presents her with a spectacle sufficiently inhumane and repulsive to weaken her hold on her own self-awareness.

The burning of the house offers us another prefigurement. It is a dramatic enough in itself but it is also the background for a magnificently arresting visual trope. The house boasts a tame parrot – Antoinette's mother's pet. Its wings have been clipped to keep it housebound. Unable to fly, it is suddenly there on the railings of the house's raised glacis, its plumage smouldering. It has no alternative. Squawking in agony it commits itself to the element that will no longer sustain it aloft and plummets to a fiery death.

Rhys obviously is preaching to the converted here, and to good immediate effect. But not entirely deftly. She has only somewhat clumsily brought the parrot's existence to our attention a page earlier. If she had brought it into the narrative far higher upstream, its symbolic value might have been far more multi-layered. Pecking spitefully at the young Antoinette's ankles – as was its wont – it would have stood for the mindlessly hostile enigma of the universe the child was awakening to; usurping her mother's affection, it would have underscored the emotional deprivation she routinely endured. To chide authors for what they have not included in a finished work is not, I imagine, a particularly valuable or even a gentlemanly practice. Most omissions are intentional and positive. Rhys' parrot, however, I would argue, indicates that she was capable on occasion of being too intent on narrative momentum.

The arson attack brings a second, more substantial figure than a parrot to the centre of our attention – Aunt Cora, sister to Antoinette's late father. A former plantation owner in her own right, Aunt Cora is disliked by the stepfather, and with good enough reason. She is both intelligent and honourable. As such, she is close enough to being unique in the entire canon of Jean Rhys' work. She is a well-off person possessing social authority who is to be admired.

Aunt Cora has her head screwed on the right way. It is her holding on to her nerve and facing down the rioters that preserves the 'gentry' from personal harm: and she has already accurately foreseen that the natives are restless. She tartly puts the insouciantly stupid stepfather in his place when he upbraids her for being alarmist:

> 'Live here most of your life and know nothing about the people. It's astonishing. They are children – they wouldn't hurt a fly.'
> 'Unhappily children do hurt flies,' said Aunt Cora.

Similarly, knowing that Antoinette's mercenarily arranged marriage to this Rochester must end in tears, Aunt Cora is not backward in berating Richard Mason on the inadequate legal provision being made for his half-sister. The stepbrother indignantly blusters:

> '… Why should I insist on a lawyer's settlement when I trust him? I would trust him with my life.'
> 'You are trusting him with her life, not yours.'

These two exchanges are two direct echoes, reworkings of an actual exchange that Jean Rhys reports in her memoir that her Dominican-born mother had with her Welsh father. A clear distinction – most importantly – must be made here. To the reader concerned with the text of the shaped novel this source is totally irrelevant. To the student of literature concerned with the springs and the limitations of creation, it may be eloquently pertinent. The source may explain why the passage is there in the text. It does not at all automatically guarantee that the passage is effective.

… Meanwhile let us return to Aunt Cora. Her purpose in the narrative is to set a compass-bearing. She is, so to speak, the amiably authoritative father figure Antoinette has never been fortunate enough to know. But Aunt Cora's absence from Jamaica for health reasons has separated the two. If Aunt Cora had been more constantly on hand as a pillar of support, Antoinette might have achieved a long, a sane and a happy life.

The firing of Antoinette's dysfunctional home occurs in her later childhood. Though they contain significant detail, Jean Rhys has her recount her convent education and adolescence in the compass of comparatively few pages. The narrative moves swiftly on to the mercenary 'courtship', the marriage, the honeymoon, the corrosive estrangement, as experienced and told by Rochester. Although this is her novel's longest section and the dynamics of the plot achieve momentum and impact within it, Rhys's flair for economical implication still delivers a pregnant brevity rather than prolonged, thoroughgoing exposition. Once again she trusts her reader to accept that a swift, loaded nod is as good as, is better than, a drawn-out wink and her contribution to the understanding is often in part that gift for an almost poetical compression. "One afternoon", she has Rochester confess to us, "the sight of a dress which she'd left lying on her bedroom floor made me breathless and savage with desire." That's all she wrote and – note the "breathless" – all she needed to.

A quick overview of the structure of *Wide Sargasso Sea* persuades us that it is divided into three parts; the first and third told from Antoinette's viewpoint, the second from Rochester's. In practice this is not quite so. Rochester's narrative has rather gawkily sandwiched in its midst a switch-back to Antoinette's point of view. (This is because the reader needs to be told that, desperate to keep her husband's love, Antoinette has to acquire an *obeah* witchcraft aphrodisiac from Christophine, the erstwhile family cook: Rochester must not and so cannot know of this.) We know from her 1950s correspondence that the viewpoint, content and structuring of the novel's central section caused Rhys more creative agony and rewriting than either the first or third and we learn too that within it this brief switch-back to

Antoinette's standpoint appeared the thorniest structural problem of all. Simply by only providing minimal clues that such a switch has occurred – yet again she chooses almost to flatter her readers as to their intelligence – Rhys just about succeeds in avoiding bringing on an epidemic of Wimbledon neck.

But in fact it might be argued the novel has five narrators. At the opening of the last section the narrative regales us with a verbatim soliloquy delivered by Grace Poole, Antoinette's Thornfield Hall gaoler. It is a delicious cameo and there in part as an *homage* to Charlotte Brontë. The manner in which Grace Poole transmutes Jane Eyre's 'Mrs Fairfax' to 'Mrs Eff' is the most delicate of valencies with which to acknowledge a debt. But the cameo is brilliantly functional too. It makes it perfectly clear why Grace Poole will prove so ineffectual as a warden. And, in admitting to another reason other than the good wages for her taking the dour job, Grace Poole, this minor character, utters a sentiment which, sadly, sat at the centre of Jean Rhys' sense of existence – possibly because it is true:

> After all the house is big and safe, a shelter from the world outside which, say what you like, can be a black and cruel world to a woman.

Grace Poole believes, mistakenly, that Thornfield Hall will provide her with a room in which she can hide from the wolves.

The brief Grace Poole vignette gives the lie to any thought that because the prose style of both Antoinette Cosway's and Rochester's narratives is close to identical, Jean Rhys could write only in one key. That she was a superb mimic is confirmed by the 'voice' of the novel's fifth narration, which comes in the form of two letters addressed to Rochester by the man who may be Daniel Boyd or Daniel Cosway and so, perhaps, possibly, probably, Antoinette's half-brother. The style and tone of these letters – as, indeed, his later dialogue face to face with Rochester – give us the poor, miserable, malignant, self-seeking wretch's entire personal tragedy in an eloquent couple of pages.

We have seen that this Jamaica has the look of a Rousseauesque Eden. But by the time the first letter is delivered we have already learned that there are snakes in this Eden, lurking giant and ancient crabs, inter-tribal hatred, *obeah* black magic, inbred insanity, an almost universal deceit. Rochester comes to learn this lesson too.

Lost in the physical transports of his early honeymoon love-making he may passingly delude himself that he is in Paradise after all. But out of the woodwork of the past comes this cut-price Iago of a Serpent. The poisoning apple he bears is the revelation, the knowledge of, certain incontrovertible home truths.

Daniel Cosway is ravaged and riven by bitterness. With good reason. The bastard mulatto son of *some* plantation owner, he has been born and brought up into no man's land. He has been given a degree of literacy and culture (the letter Rhys pens for him brilliantly defines to what inadequate limits) but no future his disgruntled spirit now thinks worthy of himself. This time it is the Iago who is without 'occupation'. Daniel Cosway – and it is his own tragedy – is, in fact, a male cousin to those protagonists of Rhys' earlier novels walking their increasingly more desperate streets. Like them, he is driven to clutching at passing chances, main or otherwise, and here may be one: quite illogically – all Roseau knows what he knows – he attempts to blackmail ("You believe me, but you want to do everything quiet like the English can") the man he alleges is his half-brother-in-law. The blackmail, for all its exorbitant level makes him repugnantly cheapskate. But we may, possibly, detect in his behaviour that element of motivated malignity which fractionally redeems it.

Above all, though, Daniel Cosway's approaching Rochester is a another necessary plot device. It is the hinge upon which a door swings open. What lies beyond is a world of deceit. Rochester does indeed believe Cosway. He is sure now that the Masons, father and son, deceived him by default in withholding from him the true nature of his wife-to-be's provenance. He knows she lied to him when, because instructed to, she told him her mother had died when she was a child and, by omission, in denying him knowledge of her relationship with another mulatto who, most like, is another bastard half-brother. Antoinette knows that Rochester lied to her in saying he loved her: he has not proved to be the stay and support she has never known. She remembers that her stepfather lied to her mother when he promised, constantly, that he would indeed arrange for her to go away "for a change". Deceit, doubt, bad faith are everywhere. Daniel Cosway does not know, finally, who his father is. He calls himself Cosway, others call him Daniel Boyd. Somebody is wrong. And if Rochester has married in bad faith it is on an island of Bad Faith. The local *obeah* holds most of the population in superstitious awe: but they hedge their bets by paying tokenesque service to the (lax) Catholicism that their former owners brought with their invasion. Jean Rhys had not spent time sitting at Ford Madox Ford's good and soldierly feet for nothing. Her Dominica-Jamaica is an island of ambiguities, and few of its inhabitants trust the intelligence those around them offer. If Daniel Cosway, albeit armed with rather more *bona fide* intelligence, is an unsubtle Iago then, by extension, Rochester is a white Othello. But another Shakespearian play may be invoked. *Macbeth* takes place in a welter of double-dealing darkness and murk. Roseau lies under the blaze of a tropical sun. But as Antoinette has sensed, it is a place where there is darkness at noon. It is close to the core of Jean Rhys' purpose that her novel adumbrates a place, a world, the human condition perhaps, where those who prosper are those best able to deceive self and neighbour alike.

His mind poisoned or his self-esteem piqued, Rochester does not return home to strangle his Desdemona. He proceeds progressively to humiliate her. He rejects her body and, more devastatingly yet, rejects her very self. Grimly, sardonically, he ceases to use the true signifier of that self, her true and musical name of Antoinette, and calls her instead by the name fastened upon her by her stepfather – Bertha. This lumpish vocative makes for a brutal bludgeoning. It designates Antoinette as his chattel. Jean Rhys, christened Ella Williams at birth, had recourse to various aliases during her chequered career. Perhaps it was from a remembered sense of a humiliating loss of identity that instead of continuing to allow her to be identified by her true, tongue-trippingly Lolitaesque name, she has Rochester inflict this dreadful European spondee – Bertha! – upon Antoinette. It is ugly, indeed, in impact. It is a beautifully judged and imaginative writer's detail.

More directly brutal still is Rochester's reaction to the aphrodisiac Antoinette administers to him in his wine. Its effect is immediate. "I remember putting out the candles on the table near the bed and that is all I remember," he says later. "All I will remember." Which is to say he remembers only too well. He has sadistically raped Antoinette. Rhys – who will have known about these things – delicately eschews any recourse to fully frontal detail but she leave us in no doubt as to what has taken place.

Rape of a worse sort follows. The following evening Rochester makes uninhibited, laughing love to Amélie, the household's young, sly, sex-pot of a maid. Antoinette, the honeymoon bride, is in the next room forced to hear everything as she lies awake the whole night long. Rochester lies with Amélie and ricocheting around in his head is a suspicion born of the pervasive island ambiguity. Could it be – it is not impossible – that Antoinette and Amélie are related …? He will never know. Anyway, this is a cash transaction … Receiving her *cadeau* with cool aplomb, Amélie departs for Rio, where rich men are for the taking. Thus, we may surmise, a potential further exemplar of Jean Rhys' self-destructive sisterhood, she begins a downward descent that will anticipate by the best part of a century the fate of the protagonists in the earlier novels.

A Rubicon has been crossed. Although Christophine proposes an alternative that might promise a less than tragic resolution, she has not enough control, egos are at too crossed purposes, for it to be pursued. The wind has become bleakly set for Thornfield Hall and the claustrophobic oblivion of the attic.

And yet … a further Shakespearian play may be evoked. Rhys has made it clear that in their initial sensual rapture both honeymooners found in each other's bodies an escape from their uncertainties and fears and doubts. A potential was there as well. Had they not been star-crossed, a love-match might have taken root. Remembering their last hours on Jamaica, Rochester acknowledges that lost potential:

I shall never understand why, suddenly, bewilderingly I was certain that everything I had imagined to be truth was false. False. Only the magic and the dream are true.

It is not slapdash to ascribe to Antoinette's fate the status of tragedy. Neither she nor Rochester, it is true, are persons of huge eminence and moral force who through fatal flaws experience a catastrophic nemesis. But then neither were Romeo and Juliet.

Once Antoinette is brought to England, Jean Rhys executes the final section of her novel with appropriate dispatch. The brief 'soliloquy' from Grace Poole has adroitly bridged time and space, and Rhys knows that henceforward prolongment should be no part of her design. Antoinette is oblivious now of time passing. And to strive for suspense would be ludicrously misconceived. Implicit in the conception of *Wide Sargasso Sea* is the certainty that the reader must have long since known its conclusion. Rhys takes us to this end with no undue haste but commendable momentum.

Her patterning of these final pages is admirably deft in two respects worthy of comment. In the first regard, without any recourse to obtrusive mechanics, she briefly solves the recurrent literary problem of how to conclude narrative unfolded in the first person of a central character who dies. Her device is a dream. Antoinette dreams her arsonist's suicide for us in a dress rehearsal of a reverie which, with delicate poignance reprises all she has lost. It is just as she steps out for the real, the live, performance, that Rhys leaves her. Thus, with a kind of logic that we can readily accept, she has left her heroine world enough and time in which to set down her tale.

More importantly, in distancing Antoinette's fiery death within the soft-edged framework of a dream – Bertha's original death, let us remember, occurs off-stage – Rhys spares us and, in a sense, her heroine the raw shock of physical reality. We have seen the parrot, Coco's, downward plunge and are happy to see no more.

As in concluding she most directly connects to the novel which inspired her, Jean Rhys allows us to remember that as a child and young girl, beset round by two faiths fixated on the morbid, Antoinette was more than once half in love with the easeful Death that would allow her to rest in peace. As always this is entirely by design. Jean Rhys ends her novel with the most delicately calculated of dying falls.

* * *

We may say with total assurance that Jean Rhys was a more accomplished novelist than Charlotte Brontë. She had enjoyed the benefit, after all, of writing at a far later stage in the collective development of the novel. Able to look back upon a long tradition – able, indeed, to benefit from *Jane Eyre* – she had the benefit of literal hindsight. There was never any danger of her committing the sort of apprentice *bêtises* that Charlotte Brontë was capable of at almost any given moment.

Jane Eyre is in many regards a thoroughly inept and almost ham-fisted performance. Its plotting depends quite outrageously upon the grossest coincidences. (Jane, close to starving in the middle of nowhere, blunders not only upon Good Samaritans but kith and kin. Her poverty-stricken fortune is altered at a stroke by a legacy from out of the blue.) Because, like a promising sixth-former who has swallowed a dictionary, Charlotte Brontë – in complete contradistinction to Jean Rhys – believes that long and Latinate words are elegantly impressive, she gives us phrases and expressions such as 'cicatrised visage' when she means 'scarred face' *passim*. Unlike Jean Rhys whose landscapes and scene-painting are always charged with subtext, are always relevantly *dramatic*, Charlotte Brontë, on occasion, offers up picturesque scenes for no better reason than that she imagines that Wordsworth will enjoy them; that this is what you are supposed to do.

And yet … too late in the tradition to be an Ur-novel, too early and written from so peripheral a cultural outpost to avoid such blemishes, *Jane Eyre* has nevertheless endured. Rightly so. Somehow its heart is in the right place.

That this is the case is, I would believe, because Charlotte Brontë has succeeded in presenting us with an entirely convincing, three-dimensional portrait of a heroine – a heroine reflecting her own author's response to existence both as directly and as subtly as Jean Rhys' protagonists reflect hers. The attitudes are, of course, 180 degrees opposed to each other; are chalk and cheese. Jane Eyre is a heroine who, under pressure, retains a calm grace and can, in every sense, remain on her own two feet. She has the inner resource to cope with life's little and not-so-little vicissitudes.

It is Charlotte Brontë's ability to make convincing her heroine's resolute but scrupulously moral tough-mindedness that has given *Jane Eyre* its lasting resonance. There is a quality of assurance about Charlotte Brontë's conception – she at least, heaven knows, did not want for a father figure! – which allows her to flesh out a fictional sensibility that triumphantly rises above all the prejudicial pitfalls implicit in her era's perception that the female was the 'gentler' sex. Wherever she has succeeded in manoeuvring Jane past the novelettish contrivances into a situation of adult confrontation or stress, the prose, the dialogue, gather impetus. The fustian falls away and we are in the presence of a proto-suffragette, a humanist reformer, a person who sets individual merit before unthinking conformity to social custom. As Charlotte Brontë's Rochester has the sense and sensibility to see, Jane Eyre is Elizabeth Bennett born into an absence of money. Without Jane Eyre on the page we might not have had George Eliot or Virginia Woolf at their desks. Or, of course, Jean Rhys.

Jane Eyre is thus an important compass bearing in our cultural history. Its many clumsinesses, its comparative lack of intellectual depth and psychological nuance doubtless preclude its being accorded the masterpiece status of *Our Mutual Friend* or *The Possessed*. But for all that, it is, very arguably, a major work. It has that landmark factor. If Charlotte Brontë had not written it, somebody else would have had to.

Jean Rhys' work, by contrast, may be called classic – 'classic' in the Louis Armstrong definition of the term that if you roll something down a hill and nothing breaks off, classic is what it is. Her punctuation – casual to a sometimes misleading fault – apart, Jean Rhys' first four novels come amazingly close to being blemish-free. They are polished in their beautifully cadenced prose and unostentatiously compact in their economy of description and use of implication. There is something of the quality of good jewellery in their manufacture.

But, if so, the stones are semi-precious. Rhys' pre-World War II novels cannot be classified as 'major'. They are too lacking in amplitude. They resonate in a minor key. As Jean Rhys would have been most well aware, set alongside the great novels of the nineteenth century her own first four lack substance..

This is not, let me be clear, for any such coarse generic reason as that their protagonists are semi-professional tarts. The Sashas and the Julias are human beings deserving of the same understanding and comparison we would accord a Jane Eyre coming to learn that Rochester had died in the vain attempt to save his wife. But in such a case Jane, in however muted a fashion, would have coped as ably as the heroine of *Villette*. Jean Rhys' Sasha Jensen and her 'sisters' have no such capability.

Essentially it is a question of intelligence. For all their streetwise know-how, these sad *demi-mondaines* lack the inner resource, the self-assurance conferred by that kind of intelligence born of secure instruction in childhood. As youth and luck ran out they became left with only the thinnest and shallowest of options. They have not the intelligent depth of character to change their losing game. Fate even denies their deriving stature from the scale of their misfortunes. To them, hapless, it makes no difference but, as Jean Rhys wants us to realise, their descent is brought about by mean wants and shortfalls rather than by epic, dignity-conferring disaster. That is the entire point.

Jean Rhys knew the parameters of her target perfectly well. As do nearly all authors, she knew when she embarked upon what became *Quartet* that she would be working in a minor theme in a minor key. We must not upbraid her for writing the book that she intended rather than the one we imagine we might prefer. And a decade after beginning *Quartet* she must have had the personal satisfaction of knowing that, minor in scale and scope though they were, she had crafted four novels of near-perfect workmanship – in the case of *Good Morning, Midnight* perhaps entirely so.

Are these remarks, then, by way of preface to remarking upon a last triumphant transposition into a resoundingly major key? The final judgement has surely to be that, no, this is not the case. Certainly the hint that Charlotte Brontë threw to Jean Rhys across a century effected a very distinct widening of the horizons not only of space and time but of characterisation as well. Antoinette with her half-sense of parallel worlds and afterlives, her bruised, attenuated relationship with the mother she so resembles, is a subtler, more deeply established and, yes, more intelligently sensitive heroine than any of her predecessors. Equally, Rhys' Rochester is not only far more of a hard-nosed bastard than Charlotte Brontë's, he is, since we see him from within, more complex and comprehensible – a far more created figure than any of the eye-for-the-main-chance, last-straw males those earlier Rhys protagonists find themselves reduced to. Indeed, reading between the lines of the narrative that Rhys puts into his mouth, we are able to glean that Jamaica has proved to be the crossroads in Rochester's life where he made the irrevocably wrong decision. As he stepped off the boat he was still possessed of worthy sensibilities and hence the potential to find a positive fulfilment. In the event he comes to emerge as an extreme instance of a young man marred by marrying too young. It is not difficult to imagine his life beyond the boundaries of his last words to us when he has rejected not only Antoinette but 'the stupid boy' who also loves him. Thornfield Hall will be his prison too.

And so too with Christophine, the *obeah* cook from sophisticated Martinique. Perceptive, clever, her skin not only black but remarkably thin, she is in no way the sister stereotype of Anna Morgan's shallow fellow chorus girls. Christophine is the novel's one survivor, and although her spirit may be corroded by her the enhanced contempt for his kind that Rochester has given her, that spirit is nevertheless still sustained by her sense of her own capabilities and worth. When, banished by Rochester, Christophine walks away without looking back, we can readily enough project that survival upon her future.

Wide Sargasso Sea, then, is clearly more expansive, less hermetically sealed within the will-paralysing meannesses of the earlier novels. Can it be said then to refute these pages' opening charge that Jean Rhys was deficient in imagination? I think not. Writ wider and more exotic it is: but once Rhys had had the wit to see that Bertha Mason's history was, *mutatis mutandis*, her own, all else was prefabricatedly there for her. She had no need for invention. The lush setting, the patois, the superstitious faiths, the latently seething hatred of black for the incompetently complacent 'white niggers', the extreme vulnerability of an unsupported girl with intelligence and feelings but no resources – all of these elements had long lain there marinating in her memory. All she had to do was access them.

All she had to do! All she had to do was structure and organise and, considered word following considered word, *write* a novel of most exquisite shape and poignant impact. Herein lie two personal triumphs.

Jean Rhys in the most important respect of all did not resemble her early heroines. She did have inner resource. There can be few, if any, more heroic examples of a writer fighting the world – a sick old age, grinding poverty, alcoholism, clenching cold, loneliness, universal oblivion – than Jean Rhys, the novelist, refusing to throw down her pen and rise from her desk, refusing to stop polishing and refining this work of her own making and spun from her own being. Grace under pressure is easy in comparison with persevering loyalty to what you believe in in an oubliette. A perseverance on to triumph.

For a triumph is what *Wide Sargasso Sea* most manifestly is. Yes, it cannot be called a masterpiece, a major work when measured against *Our Mutual Friend* because, no less manifestly, it lacks that triumph's universality. Jean Rhys did not write a novel about a Jewish girl orphaned by but surviving World War II who, hidden by a homosexual French school teacher ... You know how it goes on. However briefly, however lame the execution turned out to be, a work on such a potentially broad canvas would have had at its outset, the potential to be as awesomely commanding and profound as Dickens' two greatest novels. But, lacking that imaginative ability to think beyond her own experience, Jean Rhys was restricted to refashioning that raw – in every sense – material of her own memories.

And from this limitation perhaps her greatest achievement. She is possibly the finest example of any novelist taking the stuff of her own life and, in re-working it, transcending reminiscence into pure art. With Proust, to come full circle, with Anthony Powell, with Waugh, with the George Eliot of *Adam Bede*, with countless (lesser) others, there are those occasional passages where we are alienated by a distinct sense of being served up those warmed-over moments of autobiography. Jean Rhys never sank to such laziness or ego. Whenever she took out a memory from its pigeon-hole, she turned it about in the forefront of her intelligence and by reshaping it, by reanimating it with a word or a cadence on the page, took care to see it *worked* its passage.

This is not always immediately obvious. The economy of expression, the pregnancy of image and the consequent rapidity of progression Jean Rhys achieved make it possible to read any of her novels as if it might be no more than an extended anecdote. Indeed, given its element of being a variation on a theme, *Wide Sargasso Sea* might appear to a superficial reader scarcely more than an antique precursor of one of our contemporary urban myths. I hope I have pre-empted any such overhasty conclusion. Every novelist writes two books. The one that the reader reads first; the same book that the reader reads a second time. Few writers of fiction have produced work eliciting such pleasurably deep secondary appreciation as, thanks to her controlled local precision of means and effect, Jean Rhys managed on our behalf.

Conjoined with that last factor – because of it, indeed – let me repeat the most telling praise that she deserves. Unlike their protagonists each of her novels is self-sufficient. To appreciate, to enjoy – if that is the word – any of them we do not need to know a single detail of the author's life. No less than with the utterly anonymous Homer it is the words down there before us on the page that count.

Wide Sargasso Sea is not a masterwork. But it is a wonderfully fabricated and polished artefact. It might be compared to a Fabergé casket. One, of course, containing ashes.

As their fortunes decline, all five of Jean Rhys' heroines paradoxically go up in the world. Their attenuating fate consigns them to the meanest, cheapest rooms – the attics at the top of the ever more shabby flights of stairs in the increasingly dubious hotels. Antoinette Cosway last lays her head down to sleep in not only an attic but a prison.

Jean Rhys did not die forgotten in an attic. Through tenacity she had, in her own fine phrase, earned her death. Through her tenacity and her talent. Honour to her memory. Peace to her shade.

* * *

Bibliography

This short study will not have achieved its purpose if it has failed to convey the conviction that the best 'wider reading' in a study of Jean Rhys is to reread (the Pernod *fils* factor always borne in mind!) the novels regularly.

Rhys' own fragment of autobiography, *Smile Please* (Andrew Deutsch, 1979) is there, however, as a source of information about her earlier years and, indeed, the moment she took to writing. It is, however, a hugely sanitised source. It conveniently forgets to convey that Rhys had it in her to be the neighbour from hell for long periods of her life, and indeed the wife from hell as well. Just as she is disingenuous about her expulsion from the Academy of Dramatic Art, so, I suspect, she could not progress the memoir into that second half of her life when humiliations came upon her thick and fast. Nevertheless, *Smile Please* is compellingly illuminating about those two first decades which were to inform her fiction for ever.

A compilation of Jean Rhys' letters, *Jean Rhys: Letters 1931-66* (Andrew Deutsch, 1984; Penguin, 1985) was made available to the general public by Francis Wyndham (who most honourably championed her cause, sustained her morale and gave her money in her declining years) and Diana Melly. This correspondence, of course, comes to supply further fragments of autobiography and, when its paragraphs are read between the lines, to imply still more. In particular, the letters provide a grim insight into Rhys' long travails in bringing forth *Wide Sargasso Sea*. They give an indication of her shifting its architectural structuring over several versions and consequently a species of proleptic critical apparatus, so to speak, on the final text.

Not at all shirking the 'warts and all' refusal to collude in any cosmetic touching up, Carole Angier's *Jean Rhys: Life and Work* (André Deutsch, 1990) is the biographical corrective to *Smile Please*. In terms of its investigation of the 'Life' it may be described as less a monumentally well-conducted piece of academic research than as an exemplary piece of forensic detective work. As such it is entirely to be commended and – given that the fiction has all been read first – essential reading. For the facts this is, in effect, the primary source.

To my mind, however, the 'Work' side of Angier's study is less happy. I doubt that I quarrel with very much of her attribution of symbol and oblique meaning to Rhys' images and settings and 'props', but perhaps that very same zeal for forensic analysis has Angier anatomising the life out of the texts as she dissects them on the mortuary slab. For me at least Jean Rhys' most important characteristic – that she worked through suggestion, inference, *implicit* image: through, in fact, a poet's magic – is amputated from the corpus. See what you think.

Lorna Sage's collection of essays on twentieth-century women writers (*Moments of Truth*, Fourth Estate, 2002) includes a short analysis of *After Leaving Mr. Mackenzie*. Although Sage's cast of mind arguably imputes to Rhyss writing a more consciously cerebral process than was perhaps the case, her own sound instincts take her – and so us – close to the heart of Rhys' world and purpose.

Well worth reading in its own right, the "well-washed" (as Jean Rhys called her) Stella Bowen's own memoir *Drawn from Life* (Collins, 1941: Virago, 1984) provides an acidulous sketch of her temporary rival for Ford Madox Ford's affections that not only suggests that his real-life primary mistress may have been less complacent than her *alter ego* in *Quartet*, but that the 1920s Jean Rhys was already sufficiently possessed of the stern inner stuff that would sustain her in the face of the onslaughts later life was to visit upon her. However you referee the immediate contest both ladies have to be held to stand high in the Pantheon of twentieth-century cultural heroines.

More academic biographies and/or critical studies that may serve a turn and even further appreciation of the texts include:

L. James, *Jean Rhys*, (1978)
T. Staley, *Jean Rhys*, (1979)
P. Wolfe, *Jean Rhys*, (1980)
D. Plante, *Difficult Women*, (1983)
T. F. O'Connor, *Jean Rhys: The West Indian Novels*, (1986)
S. Bernstock, *Women of the Left Bank*, (1987)

GREENWICH EXCHANGE BOOKS

STUDENT GUIDE LITERARY SERIES

The Greenwich Exchange Student Guide Literary Series is a collection of essays on major or contemporary serious writers in English and selected European languages. The series is for the student, the teacher and 'common readers' and is an ideal resource for libraries. The *Times Educational Supplement* praised these books, saying, "The style of [this series] has a pressure of meaning behind it. Readers should learn from that ... If art is about selection, perception and taste, then this is it."

(ISBN prefix 978-1-871551 applies unless marked*, when the prefix 978-1-906075 applies.)

The series includes:
Antonin Artaud by Lee Jamieson (98-3)
W.H. Auden by Stephen Wade (36-5)
Honoré de Balzac by Wendy Mercer (48-8)
William Blake by Peter Davies (27-3)
The Brontës by Peter Davies (24-2)
Robert Browning by John Lucas (59-4)
Lord Byron by Andrew Keanie (83-9)
Samuel Taylor Coleridge by Andrew Keanie (64-8)
Joseph Conrad by Martin Seymour-Smith (18-1)
William Cowper by Michael Thorn (25-9)
Charles Dickens by Robert Giddings (26-9)
Emily Dickinson by Marnie Pomeroy (68-6)
John Donne by Sean Haldane (23-5)
Ford Madox Ford by Anthony Fowles (63-1)
The Stagecraft of Brian Friel by David Grant (74-7)
Robert Frost by Warren Hope (70-9)
Patrick Hamilton by John Harding (99-0)
Thomas Hardy by Sean Haldane (33-4)
Seamus Heaney by Warren Hope (37-2)
Joseph Heller by Anthony Fowles (84-6)
Gerard Manley Hopkins by Sean Sheehan (77-3)
James Joyce by Michael Murphy (73-0)